A BOLSHOI BALLERINA

Natalia Bessmertnova

A BOLSHOI BALLERINA

Natalia Bessmertnova

Alexander Demidov

Translated from the Russian by
Yuri S. Shirokov

Macdonald

A *Macdonald* BOOK

© Alexander Demidov 1986
Translated by Yuri Shirokov

First published in Great Britain in 1986
by Macdonald & Co (Publishers) Ltd
London & Sydney

A member of BPCC plc

British Library Cataloguing in Publication Data

Demidov, Alexander
    A Bolshoi ballerina, Natalia Bessmertnova.
    1. Bessmertnova, Natalia   2. Ballet
    dancers—Soviet Union—Biography
    I. Title
    792.8'092'4   GV1785.B45
    ISBN 0-356-12367-7

Typeset by Leaper & Gard Ltd, Bristol

Printed and bound in Great Britain by
Purnell Book Production Ltd
Member of the BPCC Group
Paulton, Bristol

Cover photography: Alexander Makarov
Editor: Catherine Rubinstein

Macdonald & Co (Publishers) Ltd
Greater London House
Hampstead Road
London NW1 7QX

Contents

Natalia Bessmertnova at home.

Preface

In the twentieth century six ballerinas have marked significant stages of progress in Russian ballet. Each of them was closely involved in innovative quests that laid the groundwork for further development of the art. Each of them expressed in dance ideas and sentiments prevailing in society rather than confining herself to a narrow, technical professional sphere.

The legendary Anna Pavlova indisputably holds pride of place among them. Although she had been raised in the strict canons of the St Petersburg style of ballet, she lent greater emotional freedom to dance, widened its imagery, and made it more expressive. Without breaking with the academic tradition, she searched for a new type of dance and intuitively linked Michel Fokine's choreographic innovations with the aesthetic principles of Marius Petipa's nineteenth-century ballet. Pavlova gave an impetus to a renovation of the classical language of dance and showed a variety of ways to interpret it.

Anna Pavlova was closely followed by Olga Spesivtseva and Marina Semenova. Spesivtseva danced in Russia for a few years before she resettled abroad in 1924. At a time of heated debates about the future of choreography and the necessity of ballet art for the new Soviet audiences, she confidently led the way as the prima ballerina of the former Marinsky Theatre, and greatly contributed to the preservation of the rich classical heritage and the classical tradition itself. Spesivtseva's dancing linked two different epochs. In a series of brilliant parts she created images of immortal beauty opposed to violence and destruction. A great tragic ballerina, she revived the style of romantic ballet with its dream of an ideal and longing for beauty. Following in Pavlova's footsteps, she enriched classical dance with expressive lines reflecting the great social upheavals of the time.

Marina Semenova joined the company (known as the Kirov Ballet today) in 1925. A strictly classical ballerina, the best pupil of Agrippina Vaganova, she introduced new qualities into classical dance — triumphant intonations, ebullient energy, heroic motifs, broad and free movement. At the same time, Semenova's forceful and joyful dancing, reflecting the constructive spirit of the late 1920s, remained faithful to the classical style. This was a fundamental feature of her art. At a time of attacks against Petipa and Tchaikovsky, when classical dance was sometimes rejected out of hand, her approach vividly demonstrated the unlimited possibilities of the classical style and, more importantly, its consonance with the spirit of the day in the new social situation.

The key to the next stage was Galina Ulanova's style of dancing. The success of the ballet theatre in the 1930s and 1940s was largely due to her brilliant performances, and she stimulated interest in serious literature and drama. A classical ballerina of the Leningrad school, she presented striking specimens of profound creativity. Her parts were remarkable for their psychological precision and emotional veracity.

The daring and defiant art of Maya Plisetskaya marked a radical change in public sentiments during the 1950s and 1960s. A ballerina of unique natural endowments, she remained loyal to the traditions of the classical school but never limited herself to its stringent prescriptions. She declared her creed for all to see in her spectacular dancing, upholding a world outlook that rejected dogma and affirmed free thinking and unorthodoxy as essential principles for the creative individual.

The 1970s and 1980s are the era of Natalia Bessmertnova, of new genres of ballet and a new period in its development — marked primarily by the productions of Yuri Grigorovich, chief choreographer of the Bolshoi.

Bessmertnova is a Muscovite, as is Plisetskaya. After the War the focus of ballet life in the Soviet Union moved from Leningrad to Moscow. Both Semenova and Ulanova continued and completed their careers there.

Bessmertnova's art has absorbed Spesivtseva's romanticism, Pavlova's musical expressiveness, the broad dancing of Semenova and Ulanova's lyricism. It has developed at the junction of different traditions but in the mainstream of a school of dance common to all of them. It has accumulated the experience of different generations and has been influenced by the distinctive Moscow school of dance, prone to heroic exaltation with a vivid dramatic element. Bessmertnova's art is the culmination of the ballet dancing of the twentieth century, and can be traced back to the romantic ballets of Taglioni and Grisi. Her dancing stands out in salient relief, even against the background of her celebrated predecessors, for its individuality and originality, consonant with the public sentiments and moods of the time.

This book attempts to sum up the spectacular artistic career of Natalia Bessmertnova.

As Autumn in *Cinderella* in London on her first tour abroad.

The First Steps

Natalia Bessmertnova was born in Moscow on 19 July 1941. That day, an unusually violent storm swept the city; the deafening peals of thunder seemed to salute one of the most important events in the history of Russian ballet.

At the time Russia was deeply involved in the war against Nazi Germany, and 1941 was a particularly hard year. Not long after her birth, therefore, the baby girl was taken by her mother, Antonina Yakovlevna, to safety in Leninabad in Central Asia, while her father, Igor Borisovich, went to serve as a doctor with the fighting forces.

Natalia's real childhood was spent in Moscow, where the family was reunited shortly before V-E Day. She grew up in the cosy atmosphere of the postwar years, when life became secure and stable once more after all the hardship and privation of wartime. The climate in her home was one of affection and attention. Natalia was raised as a normal child, and her parents never regarded her as a child prodigy even when her exceptional talent became obvious.

They taught her to be hard-working and considerate, and she would willingly help her mother with the daily chores and keeping the house. When her sister Tatiana was born in 1947, Natalia was especially helpful.*

She was also encouraged to read classics. Indeed, Alexander Pushkin, the greatest of Russian poets, was idolized in the family. There was a special reason for this: her father was one of the poet's descendants. But despite their pride in their great ancestor, her parents modestly believed that no spark of his genius had been inherited by their children. They certainly never thought of a stage career for Natalia; her infatuation with dancing simply amused them.

Natalia's dancing hobby bordered on a compulsion. She could dance to any music for hours on end. She did not care if anybody was watching her — she was too young to be afflicted with stage fright, something she would have to fight off for years before finally gaining total self-control. In her dances, of course, she had only her instinct to guide her, and she followed no regular pattern that would make her efforts coherent. She simply had a penchant that longed for expression and a vague awareness of herself as a future dancer. She knew of ballet by hearsay, but that was a dream world of fairy tales.

Eventually Natalia's parents began to realize that she was born to dance, and her mother took her to dance classes at the city's Young Pioneer Palace, a cultural club for children that is found in every Soviet city. The classes were run by Helena Rosse, an ex-ballerina and an experienced teacher.

It was a hard period: Natalia had to go to school every day and also attended dance classes three times a week. Rosse was an exacting teacher and a stickler for punctuality. No slip or wrong step would escape her watchful eye. 'Difficulty is your ally. What is learned the hard way is hard to forget,' she used to tell her pupils. It was on her advice that Natalia's parents decided that she should take the entrance examination for the Moscow Ballet School.

On the day of the examination Natalia was escorted to the ballet school by her whole family. She was excited and tense with apprehension. This was her first and last chance: she was already eleven, and she knew that if she failed there would be no second attempt. Her fears, however, proved unfounded. Of the nine girls selected from 300 applicants, Natalia alone was admitted without reservations.

* * *

The life of a ballet pupil is quite unlike that of an ordinary schoolchild. In addition to the regular school curriculum, the ballet school programme contains many special subjects, such as the history of theatrical art, the costume, music and dance.

Furthermore, ballet schools are known for their strict moral rules and rigid discipline. Pupils are trained to take a professional approach from the first year of study, and there is stiff competition between them throughout their schooling. Truancy or violations of the school routine are unthinkable; laziness, misbehaviour and other faults may be penalized by immediate expulsion. Ballet schools train professional dancers, so the first principle that is driven home to pupils is that negligence means unfitness for their chosen profession.

Ballet pupils are sharply different from other children. They are usually serious, reticent and unspoiled. Their intensive training tends to affect their looks and character; a measure of asceticism is an intrinsic quality of their profession. This may account for what Margot Fonteyn once described as the 'curious pallor peculiar to so many dancers from Russia'.

* * *

Among the school's teachers of classical dance, two played particularly significant parts in Natalia's life: Maria Kozhukhova and Sophia Golovkina.

It was Kozhukhova who actually shaped Bessmertnova's style of dancing. She had been a ballerina at the Marinsky Theatre in St Petersburg and taught at the Leningrad Ballet School until she moved to Moscow in 1935. Incalcitrant by nature, she never abandoned the style she had followed for

---

*Tatiana Bessmertnova followed in her elder sister's footsteps. In 1967 she graduated from the Moscow Ballet School with flying colours and joined the Bolshoi Ballet as a soloist. Her repertoire contains many spectacular solo parts: the pas de trois and one of the Spanish brides in *Swan Lake* to Yuri Grigorovich's choreography, a street dancer in *Don Quixote*, a magnificent Myrtha in *Giselle*, a brilliant Aegina in *Spartacus*, and Zarema in *The Fountain of Bakhchisarai*. She has a strikingly individual style of dance remarkable for its charm, beauty and expressive grace.

twenty years on stage. Thus, despite being Moscow-trained, Natalia says that she belongs to the Leningrad school of academic dance.

There is a continuity of tradition in Soviet ballet. In 1915 Kozhukhova graduated from Klavdia Kulichevskaya's class at the Marinsky Theatre. The graduates from the same class two years previously had included Olga Spesivtseva, who became one of the greatest ballerinas of the twentieth century and was placed by many on a par with Anna Pavlova. Kozhukhova, who had worked at the same theatre as Spesivtseva, immediately noticed Bessmertnova's striking resemblance to her former colleague in her looks and body lines.

Kozhukhova was the first to pinpoint Bessmertnova's individuality and flair for the romantic. Nonetheless she believed that, for all the individuality of the dancer, dance technique should be impeccable — no talent can compensate for faults in execution — and in her hey-day she herself had been much admired for her superlative pirouette technique. She communicated these ideas to Bessmertnova, and they fell upon fertile soil.

After Kozhukhova's death in 1959 her class was taken over by Sophia Golovkina, the principal of the Moscow Ballet School today. She was a very different type of person: a young woman, friendly and energetic, who had left the stage only recently. Her dancing style emphasized the sensual element, with a frankness and broadness characteristic of the Moscow school of dance.

Golovkina quickly appreciated Bessmertnova's romantic charm, but also worked at polishing her virtuoso technique. She did not believe that the young ballerina was only good for lyrical parts — that would mean merely taking advantage of her good looks, belittling her true endowments as a dancer and the range of her talents. She faced her pupil with serious professional and psychological tasks in order to widen the range of parts the young ballerina would be able to perform in her future career. Bessmertnova says today that one of the most valuable results of her training under Golovkina was a feeling of confidence. This quality is indispensable on stage: there is no place in the theatre for an actor plagued by stage fright.

Between them, these two teachers provided an invaluable training: Kozhukhova identified Bessmertnova's individuality and potential and laid the groundwork for her virtuoso technique; Golovkina applied the finishing touches.

* * *

Natalia made her debut on the Bolshoi stage on 20 June 1961, when she was still a student. She danced the Seventh Waltz in *Chopiniana*. The opportunity had arisen through exigency, and she came on stage practically without having rehearsed her part. But she danced with full abandon and youthful enthusiasm, and succeeded in winning the admiration of the audience.

When she crossed the huge Bolshoi stage in a series of almost weightless, impossibly extended leaps, the audience sat breathless and then burst into stormy applause. People looked at one another in disbelief: was it really true, or was

Natalia (right) with her mother and sister.

it a miracle?

Bessmertnova's rare musicality helped to fill with inspiration the canonical movements and poses. For instance, in the pose of the 'listening sylphide', she did not bring her hand closer to her ear while listening, as other ballerinas had done. She was indeed listening, and stood motionless and concentrated, fearfully sensitive to every sound in the dream wood.

In that performance the audience saw more than a wonderful physique with the fascination of natural line and lightness. It was a sensitive representation of the style of the music and choreography, a plaintive, melancholy ephemerality, the inscrutability and inaccessibility of a choreographic dream, oblivious of routine and reality.

Thus, as often happens in the world of ballet, Natalia leapt to the public eye by a stroke of fortune. Her career accelerated immediately.

Fedor Lopukhov, an outstanding Soviet choreographer, a brilliant connoisseur of classics, and Vaclav Nijinsky's schoolmate, occasionally visited Golovkina's class and silently watched pupils in training. 'Who is that dark girl at the barre?' he asked once. The teacher explained. 'This youngster has all the makings of a star. In time she will make the world talk about her,' the old man said.

* * *

Graduation exams were held in June 1961, and the students danced in turn before a distinguished panel headed by the world-famous ballerina Galina Ulanova.

For her set pieces Natalia chose a Liszt étude and one of the variations from *Don Quixote*. This was considered an unusual and rather incompatible combination, but then the judges soon realized they were watching a very unusual talent, not just the best of the bunch, but a truly original dancer in a class of her own.

They were so much impressed by her originality and by her performance of forty-eight *fouettés* that they awarded her an almost unheard-of Grade A1, and she was immediately accepted into the Bolshoi Ballet Company. She had just turned twenty, and her steep rise to stardom had now begun.

CHAPTER TWO

The Bolshoi

Natalia Bessmertnova joined the Bolshoi Ballet Company, with its splendid traditions and great masters of the historic art, just as it was preparing to celebrate its bicentennial. It was a time of new ideas, and the Bolshoi Ballet was at a crossroads after a long period of infatuation with the dramatic, story-telling approach to ballet, which had reigned supreme on the Bolshoi stage for a good twenty-five years.

In that period the company had developed its distinctive artistic principles and its own school of dance remarkable for its athletic grace. However, despite being the country's leading theatre, the Bolshoi confined itself to imitations of the finest productions of the Kirov Ballet in Leningrad. It was only in classics, which were few and far between, that it preserved its independence, staging such masterpieces as *Swan Lake*, *The Sleeping Beauty*, *Raymonda* or *Giselle*.

In the early 1960s, when Bessmertnova made her debut on the Bolshoi stage, the company had great professional potential. It had a strong contingent of established first-class ballerinas and male dancers, Maya Plisetskaya, Raisa Struchkova and Mikhail Fadeyechev among them. All of them were in the prime of life. Moreover, between 1958 and 1961 the company had received a liberal infusion of young blood: Ekaterina Maximova, Vladimir Vasilyev, Nina Sorokina, Mikhail Lavrovsky, Nina Timofeyeva, Marina Kondratyeva, Yuri Vladimirov, Maris Liepa and Vladimir Tikhonov.

The company as a whole was young and full of enthusiasm that was searching for an outlet. The need for innovation was on everybody's lips. The company's potential was far too great for anything its choreographers could offer to bring it into play. The old classical ballets that were on the Bolshoi repertoire were in fact the main field where the dancers could show their skill and creativity. That was certainly not enough.

In the meantime, new winds were blowing on the Soviet ballet scene. New ideas arising from the innovative quests of the young choreographers Yuri Grigorovich and Igor Belsky were gaining ground at the Kirov Ballet, resulting in a revival of the rich imagery of dance, the development of its fluid language, a search for polysemantic forms of portraying reality not limited to the drab monotony of lifelikeness and the ossified dogma of 'photographic' realism. Thus the Bolshoi could offer nothing but long-familiar parts to its young dancers of a new stamp — such as Bessmertnova, Vasilyev, Lavrovsky and Maximova, to mention but a few — while at the Kirov Ballet in Leningrad, Yuri Grigorovich was rapidly coming into his own as a choreographer capable of satisfying their thirst for innovation.

As a result, in 1959 *The Stone Flower*, a ballet based on the motifs of folk tales of the Urals, to music by Sergei

Prokofiev, with Yuri Grigorovich's choreography, was transferred from the Kirov Ballet to the Bolshoi stage. The ballet hit the headlines of the American press during the company's guest tour of the United States in 1959. *The Stone Flower*, however, was an isolated event for the Bolshoi in that period.

* * *

Natalia Bessmertnova made her second, 'official' debut at the Bolshoi in *Swan Lake* at a matinée on 14 October 1961. The part of Odette-Odile, of course, was as yet a coveted but distant goal, and she appeared as a bride in the second act. That was followed by the part of one of the three swans and pas de trois in *Swan Lake*, one of the two snowflakes in *The Nutcracker*, and one of the two wilis in *Giselle*.

On December 31 she danced her first major role, that of Andrei's daughter in Andrei Balanchivadze's *Pages From Life*, Leonid Lavrovsky's unsuccessful attempt to embody a modern theme in ballet. This production was quickly dropped from the repertoire, leaving her to wonder about the vicissitudes of artistic fortune.

Her next solo part was the third variation of the Dance of the Shadows in a revival of *La Bayadère*. In the Bolshoi Ballet's guest tour of the United States and Canada, her first, she danced one of the twelve maidens in Leonid Jacobson's version of *Spartacus*, one of the three nymphs in *Walpurgis Night*, a small solo in *The Class Concert*, and one of the wilis in *Giselle*.

During the Bolshoi Ballet's guest performances in Britain in 1963, Bessmertnova was noticed in her smallest roles (Fairy Autumn in *Cinderella*, a bride in *Swan Lake*, a friend of Juliet in *Romeo and Juliet*). Critics declared that there was a strange exotic magic in her style, which could not be expressed in words but which clearly proved that a 'rare jewel' had appeared on stage. They also said that she gave a clear finish to each movement without breaking the flow, keeping a thoughtful and reserved expression on her face. Natalia Bessmertnova, they said, had a natural romantic style which could not have been learned.

Clement Crisp, the famous British critic, wrote that the whole Bolshoi company danced beautifully and that it would be unfair to single out anybody, and yet ... he would like to mention one dancer who would stand out in any ballet, no matter what and where she danced. He was referring to Bessmertnova.

On the first night, he wrote, they saw a dancer with unique talent. She was one of the three swans. Throughout the company's season all eyes were fixed on the fragile Natalia Bessmertnova and her extraordinary gracefulness (*Financial Times*, 29 July 1963).

The third season at the Bolshoi was crucial for the young ballerina. The choreographer Leonid Lavrovsky picked her

Top, the Bolshoi Ballet School. Bottom left and bottom right, Natalia as a ballet student.

Top, Natalia Bessmertnova (centre) as one of the three swans in *Swan Lake* with the Bolshoi Ballet Company in London, 1963. Bottom, with Sofia Golovkina, director of the Bolshoi Ballet School.

for the part of Giselle in his version of the ballet and it was he who helped her to bring her work on this role to a truly triumphant conclusion. After a few rehearsals he decided to allow her to dance the part as she wanted to dance it, relying on her intuition. His intervention was limited to observation and advice.

Now that she was free to come up with her own interpretation, the young ballerina felt a surge of confidence. Though she realized the risks involved in her newly gained independence, she was not afraid. This was the chance of a lifetime.

On 20 November 1963 Bessmertnova danced Giselle on the Bolshoi stage. This date can be considered to mark her emergence as a great ballerina.

Her dancing was a miracle and had a hypnotic effect on the audience. Thousands of unblinking eyes watched her every movement excitedly and gratefully. They saw the unique capacity for fluid expressiveness that lay beneath all her movements. When, in the scene of madness, her arms suddenly dropped lifelessly, all hearts ached at the sight of her infinitely sincere expression of hopeless sorrow. The unique cantilena of her flights, her light, small, *terre-à-terre* steps perfectly suited the style of the ballet.

This was partly due to her physical appearance. The audience was impressed by the beauty of her slim body and the unique expressiveness of her thin arms and long hands. She evoked recollections of the image of the famous Russian ballerina Olga Spesivtseva and her fluent yet nervous line. But over and above that, Natalia Bessmertnova conveyed great strength of spirit and an ability for self-absorption, remaining aloof from the petty and prosaic. She certainly knew how to dance as she wanted and as her emotions suggested, for her own enjoyment.

Bessmertnova recalls that event in these words: 'I had long dreamt of dancing Giselle. I felt I was good for that role. That blissful night of my first appearance as Giselle is still fresh in my memory. The sensation of weightlessness I felt then is still there, though I have danced Giselle more often than any other part. My debut in *Giselle* is the most vivid recollection of my youth. I am deeply thankful to Leonid Lavrovsky for his trust in my ability to cope with that role.'

That debut marked a turning-point in her life on both an artistic and a psychological level. In 1963 Lavrovsky was practically on the way out as the leader of the ballet company. At the close of his career he had given free rein to innovation and young talent, which was of major significance for Bessmertnova and for Russian ballet as a whole. For the young ballerina the difficulties of the formative period were now a thing of the past. She was a new star in the brilliant constellation of Bolshoi dancers.

The Bolshoi Theatre.

CHAPTER THREE

Stardom

Giselle had summed up a stage in Bessmertnova's life and work. The most important events of the next few years were her new parts: Shirin in *Legend of Love* by Arif Melikov with Yuri Grigorovich's choreography; Odette-Odile in the old, classical version of *Swan Lake*; Phrygia in *Spartacus* by Aram Khachaturian, with choreography by Yuri Grigorovich again.

'The most memorable role of that time for me is Shirin. That was the first premiere in my life. In all other parts, including Giselle, I had been just another entrant. I had danced Phrygia as a member of the second, stand-by cast. Moreover, Shirin was my first role choreographed by Grigorovich, who had come to lead the ballet company shortly before,' the ballerina recalls today. Shirin marked her second triumph after Giselle.

In the period between Giselle and Shirin, Bessmertnova had danced the Good Fairy and Princess Florina in *The Sleeping Beauty*, the Muse in *Paganini* to music by Sergei Rachmaninov in Leonid Lavrovsky's production, Maria in *The Fountain of Bakhchisarai* based on Alexander Pushkin's poem of the same name, and Leili in *Leili and Mejnun* to music by Sergei Balasanian.

The latter ballet was produced at the Bolshoi by the veteran choreographer Kasyan Goleizovsky. Bessmertnova was his favourite; he admired the young ballerina and predicted a great future for her. After the premiere he sent her a message which said: 'Natalia, you are incomparable, divine, and light as a silvery cloud with large intelligent eyes like two souls, like two icon-lamps that illumine your face. I thank you for the enormous pleasure that made me see nothing but you on the stage.'

Leili was an exquisitely beautiful and slightly mysterious character, but politely indifferent to the touchingly sentimental drama developing around her. With her unusually pliant body, the natural cantilena quality of her dancing and her lively imagination, Natalia sensed the spirit of Oriental dance as if she was made for it. The ballet had its first night in December 1964. It was a step on the way towards her triumphant success in *Legend of Love*.

Shirin

Bessmertnova danced Shirin in *Legend of Love* at its premiere at the Bolshoi on 15 April 1965. The ballet was a sensational success and exerted a great influence on the development of Soviet ballet. At that time it was an unusually topical ballet, reflecting ideas that excited the Soviet intelligentsia in the late 1950s and early 1960s.

The music for the ballet by the young Azerbaijanian composer Arif Melikov was in Oriental style and contained no discoveries in methods or forms. It was a rather traditional ballet score, melodious enough but lacking forcefulness and depth. The subject was borrowed from a drama by the Turkish poet Nazym Hikmet. It is a poetical drama based on a popular Eastern legend about the tragic love of the court artist Ferkhad for Shirin, the sister of the powerful Queen Mekhmeneh-Banu, who had earlier sacrificed her beauty to save Shirin from inevitable death.

The Queen falls in love with Ferkhad. She is in despair, because she knows that she is too ugly to expect anything but disappointment, but is unable to bring her passion under control. Her hopeless love drives her to frenzy. She forcibly separates Shirin and Ferkhad and exiles him to the mountains to dig a tunnel through the rocks that will bring water to the thirsty people of her kingdom. Ferkhad will be allowed to come back if he completes this arduous task.

After some time the Queen repents, aware that her cruelty has not made her happy. She pardons Ferkhad, inviting him to rejoin his beloved. Ferkhad, however, declines the offer. Now his life belongs to the people, his first duty is to help them and make their wish for a better life come true.

Nazym Hikmet's play, which was quite a hit at one time, was usually interpreted in a straightforward way as the priority of public over private interest. Grigorovich's choreography also brought out other, more subtle issues.

His interpretation of the subject was astute and far-sighted. He created the image of a despotic Oriental state inhabited by terrorized, ghost-like subjects obedient to the wilful rule of a tyrant. Paradoxically, the tyrant proves vulnerable to ordinary human emotions and learns that love cannot be won by imperial orders or powerful armies. The desperation of Queen Mekhmeneh-Banu, who rules the destinies of human beings, stands out in sharp contrast to the free love of the two young, stout hearts unsubdued by persecution and exile.

The relationship between Ferkhad and Shirin is not devoid of conflict, however. Shirin is a symbol of love, quiet and family life. The hero's ambitions are different and leave no place for love that conflicts with his dedication to art and his ideals. In the choreographer's philosophical conception art comes first, and love has to retreat.

Bessmertnova challenged that conception. Her apparent portrayal of Shirin as an elegiac melancholy dreamer concealed a volcano of energy, a character stubborn and wilful. She did not resign herself to her fate but put up a fight for her freedom. Ferkhad sought freedom in art, but Shirin sought freedom in love alone.

Grigorovich had visualized Shirin as a sensible girl who would understand Ferkhad's refusal to come back to her. Bessmertnova opposed this 'male' viewpoint. In the final scenes following her impassioned appeal to her beloved she displayed no admiration for Ferkhad's self-sacrifice.

As Leili in *Leili and Mejnun* in 1964.

Above, in her dressing room before a performance of *Leili and Mejnun*. Below, as Shirin in *Legend of Love* with Alexander Bogatyrev.

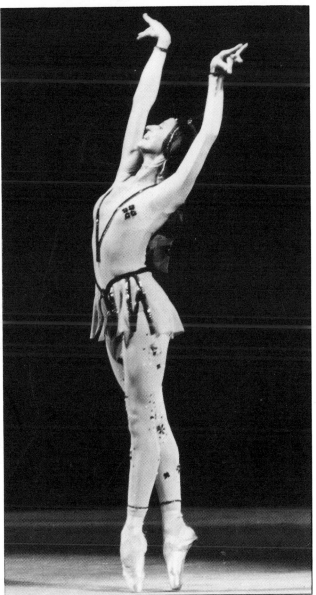

As Shirin in *Legend of Love* with Mikhail Lavrovsky.

Shirin's variations in *Legend of Love*.

As Phrygia in *Spartacus* with Irek Mukhamedov, 1984.

As Phrygia in *Spartacus*, 1984.

Dancing Phrygia in *Spartacus* with Irek Mukhamedov, 1984.

Left and above, as Phrygia in *Spartacus* with Irek Mukhamedov, 1984.

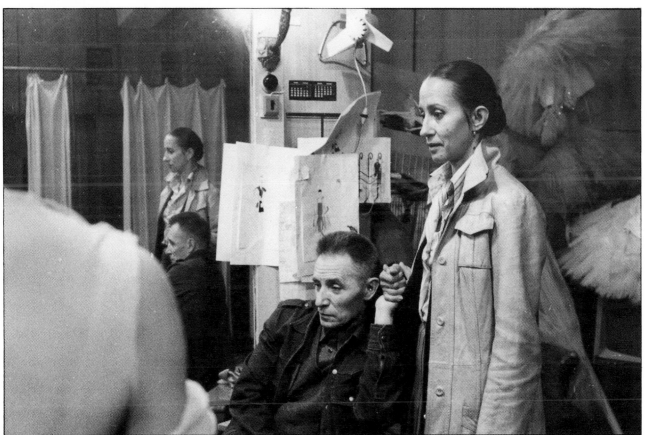

Watching the death of Spartacus with Yuri Grigorovich.

Top, Aurora's variations in *The Sleeping Beauty.* Bottom, as Aurora in *The Sleeping Beauty* with Alexander Bogatyrev.

As Aurora in *The Sleeping Beauty* with Alexander Bogatyrev.

Dancing the role of Kitri in *Don Quixote.*

As Kitri in *Don Quixote*.

Her dancing showed her revolt against the injustice of fate, her bitter reluctance to accept defeat, and her awareness of the tragedy of her dashed hopes that doomed her to loneliness.

Phrygia

Bessmertnova first danced Phrygia in *Spartacus* at the Bolshoi on 14 April 1968. In this ballet on a subject from ancient history Yuri Grigorovich presented a social confrontation between the old world and the new.

In the focus of the conflict are two characters symbolizing these two intransigent camps: the Roman patrician Crassus and the Thracian gladiator Spartacus. The powerful Rome of Crassus conquers foreign lands and subjugates free peoples to its unchallenged rule. The vanquished people, however, are not subdued; they rise in arms against their oppressors. Their rebellious spirit and hopes for freedom are expressed by Spartacus, the leader of the insurgent army of slaves.

Phrygia, who is Spartacus's wife, symbolizes the image of an ideal supportive beloved — faithful, submissive and patient. Her lot is uncomplaining attendance and complete subordination to her husband's will. The choreographer denies her a right to action, limiting her life to the joys of brief meetings with the hero between battles. She gives him rest and consolation whenever he needs them, resigning herself to waiting for the short happy moments when he finally remembers her.

In *Spartacus* Grigorovich upheld his concept of a hero seeking freedom in lofty exploits and realizing his destiny outside the sphere of private life and love, which are irrelevant to the global conflicts that constitute the action of the ballet.

Despite having accepted this type of role with a certain reluctance, Bessmertnova breathed life into the part of Phrygia, which required filigree dancing technique and acting skill. She did not emphasize sentimental details or individual poses in the scenes of the Crassus orgy or the slave market but presented Phrygia as a symbolic figure in accordance with the choreographer's conception.

She was heart-rendingly pathetic in tragic episodes and affectionately lyrical in love adagios which seemed to have been devised to match her individual style of dance, although she was not the first performer of the role. These adagios, with their flexible long lines forming a fantastic fluid pattern undisturbed by any hint of sharp motion, were the culmination of her dance. Bessmertnova showed herself for the first time as a brilliant virtuoso of duet dance.

* * *

The next stage in Bessmertnova's career lasted roughly seven years: from 1968 to 1975. Although she did not appear in any more premieres except Grigorovich's new production of *Swan Lake* in 1969, she rose to the top in the Bolshoi Ballet. Her technical skill and artistry matured and she gained greater confidence based on stable professionalism.

Her main parts now were in classical ballets, in either new or traditional versions: Masha in *The Nutcracker*, Aurora in *The Sleeping Beauty*, Kitri in *Don Quixote*, Odette-Odile in the new version of *Swan Lake*. They evidenced a sharp increase in the range of her parts. She was equally brilliant in Marius Petipa's classical version of *The Sleeping Beauty*, in the comical genre of *Don Quixote*, in the lyrical, melancholy and sinister *Swan Lake* and in the graceful puppet-show-like scenes of *The Nutcracker*.

Her finest achievements were Masha in *The Nutcracker* and Odette-Odile in *Swan Lake*. They showed her mature mastery and strikingly individual manner of dance. 'Among my parts of those years Masha was the most enjoyable one,' she recalls. 'It strengthened my faith in my fitness for intricate dance work. In *Swan Lake* I had danced before, so there were no new impressions. I danced Kitri in *Don Quixote* only on rare occasions. Aurora in *The Sleeping Beauty* had always seemed a somewhat abstract character to me. I tried to do my level best to live up to the hopes pinned on me by the choreographer and I was happy to hear commendation of my performance.'

Masha

On 16 June 1968 Bessmertnova danced the part of Masha in Tchaikovsky's *The Nutcracker* to Grigorovich's choreography at the Bolshoi. It had seemed to many that she would probably be unfit for this role since in her looks and style she was very unlike its first performers, Ekaterina Maximova and Nina Sorokina, who were close to the ingénue type. It was difficult to imagine her in the initial episodes where the heroine is still a child engrossed in her games.

Hoffmann's fairy tale and Tchaikovsky's music create an atmosphere of childish play and sincere faith in miracles. In the choreography, the part of Masha in the Christmas party scene is based on the virtuoso technique of little and graceful *par terre* movements. This style of dance was slightly at variance with Bessmertnova's own personal approach, so she sought out elements that she could relate to in her interpretation of the ballet.

The Nutcracker was Grigorovich's first original production in Moscow. It had its first night on 12 March 1966, and was, in fact, the first serious interpretation of Tchaikovsky's masterpiece. The ballet was a mystery that had not been unravelled by the last century's ballet masters and caused a lot of headache for contemporary choreographers.

Grigorovich broke with the tradition of staging *The Nutcracker* as a ballet for children interspersed with naive miracles and magical transformations, though he preserved its fairy-tale plot. In his choreography he sought to bring Tchaikovsky's music and Hoffmann's fairy tale closer to each other, excluded child dancers and reinforced the fantastic element, interpreting the score as a lyrical poem about the heroine's transition from childhood to youth.

The result was a ballet full of joy and radiance, in which the heroine achieves harmony with herself through the adventures of her dream the night after a Christmas party at which she has been given an ugly nutcracker doll. Her love and self-sacrifice save the toy from the hordes of the ferocious Mouse King, and the toy is transformed into a fine Prince who leads her into a magic world of stars where she

As Masha in *The Nutcracker* with Mikhail Lavrovsky.

Dancing Masha in *The Nutcracker* with Mikhail Lavrovsky.

gives her heart to him.

Bessmertnova immediately grasped the meaning of this transformation. It was not simply the story of a girl who lets her imagination run away but a picture of a young life at its turning-point. Masha is no longer a child at heart but has not yet parted with her childhood. This approach revealed an unexpected psychological message of the ballet.

Natalia Bessmertnova's Masha lives a dual life: one in the daytime, the other at night. As though enchanted, she descends to the dark sitting-room eager to see a new world. She dreams of freedom and a flight to the skies. Her eyes are turned upwards. Her dance little by little releases her from the grip of ordinary life.

In the scene of the night-time battle she meets the Nutcracker who is fighting the legions of the evil Mouse King. Suddenly she becomes aware of a secret link between herself and the toy warrior fighting at the head of his puppet army against overwhelming odds. Masha understands that

he needs help, love and care at the moment when he is almost overpowered by his enemies. She promptly comes to his rescue, and her courage is rewarded with her toy's transformation into a handsome and gallant Prince, symbolizing the final triumph of justice.

Natalia Bessmertnova's dancing showed Masha's implicit faith in this eventual victory of good over evil. In the finale of the ballet, when Masha awakens from her dream the Prince disappears into the darkness behind the fading candlelight. The sitting-room again appears on stage and the Nutcracker is seen again as an ugly doll. What Bessmertnova's dancing conveyed, however, was not the end of a dream. It was a dance of new hope that promised love and happiness.

It proved symbolic on a personal plane as well. In 1968 she was married to Grigorovich. As a married woman, her life acquired greater stability and she took on a new range of private concerns.

CHAPTER FOUR

Grigorovich

The Nutcracker marked the beginning of a new chapter in Bessmertnova's life and art. The keynote of this era was Grigorovich and his productions. Natalia danced parts specially created for her, though she was not, as a rule, their only performer. This stage in her career consisted of two cycles of works. The first comprised Anasthasia in *Ivan the Terrible* to music by Sergei Prokofiev, Valentina in *The Angara* by the contemporary Soviet composer Andrei Eshpai, and Juliet in *Romeo and Juliet* by Sergei Prokofiev in Grigorovich's new version. The second cycle consisted of later works: Rita in *The Golden Age*, an early ballet by Dmitri Shostakovich, and Raymonda in Alexander Glazunov's ballet of the same name.

Natalia Bessmertnova danced in the premieres of all these productions. The parts of Anasthasia, Rita and Raymonda are her best achievements to date. In Grigorovich's productions she has found a repertoire, characters and roles that harmonize with her artistic nature, psychology and world outlook. In these ballets she has been able to reveal her talent to the full.

The years from 1968 to 1979 were an eventful period of fascinating work at the Bolshoi, numerous parts in its various productions, and triumphant success abroad. Bessmertnova went on many guest tours with the Bolshoi company and performed as a visiting soloist at the world's most famous theatres: the Grand Opéra in Paris, La Scala in Milan, the Rome Opera House, the Metropolitan Opera House in New York, and London's Covent Garden, to mention but a few.

In 1969 she danced in Britain, West Germany and Poland; in 1970 in Japan, Turkey, Iran, Italy, Hungary and Yugoslavia; in 1972 in Lebanon, Syria, Norway, Sweden, Denmark, Poland and Yugoslavia; in 1972 in Norway, France and Bulgaria; in 1973 in West Germany, the USA, Japan, France and Austria; in 1974 in Egypt, Bulgaria and Britain; in 1975 in the USA and Czechoslovakia. Reviews of her performances could fill a large volume.

During the Bolshoi Ballet's guest performances in Britain in 1969 Natalia Bessmertnova appeared in four main parts: Masha, Phrygia, Giselle and Odette-Odile in the traditional version of *Swan Lake*. She also danced Shirin in the Second Act of *Legend of Love*, which was a separate item on the company's composite programme. The British press lavished praises on the young ballerina. Her success with the discriminating British ballet-lovers affirmed her status as a superstar of contemporary ballet.

Anasthasia

The role of Anasthasia in *Ivan the Terrible* was the first to be devised especially for Bessmertnova, and opened a new chapter in her artistic career. This ballet to Sergei Proko-

fiev's music deals with a subject from Russian history — the first Russian tzar, Ivan the Terrible, and his wife Anasthasia. In Russian history Anasthasia is listed in the ancestry of the Romanov royal family, to which the last Russian tzar, Nicholas II, belonged.

The part of Anasthasia was in fact a turning-point in Bessmertnova's work under Grigorovich's guidance, leading her away from classical roles. She says today that classical ballets hold much less interest for her than her new roles in Grigorovich's ballets of the last few years. She loves classics, of course, but she is not prone to blind worship of the brilliant past. 'Classics are much too general,' she says. 'Today I am more fascinated with human characters and destinies. But I have no intention of giving up the traditional repertoire and concentrating on modern ballet. Classics are necessary for any serious artist.'

Grigorovich showed a novel approach to the personality of Ivan IV, a medieval Russian monarch whose rule was marred by savage atrocities. The Tzar sought to unite Russia, uproot the vestiges of the Mongol conquest and consolidate the country territorially as a powerful state capable of challenging the greatest European powers.

During the last two centuries the figure of Ivan the Terrible has riveted the attention of various Russian artists — novelists, painters, composers and film directors. He has provided the motive for reflection on the sources and character of the Russian state and has often been the subject of heated debates between various opposing factions. He has given rise to political allusions, which have rarely taken the form of objective historical analysis. Either Ivan the Terrible has been denounced as a cruel tyrant who tortured and exiled his subjects, or his reign of terror has been vindicated by references to the supreme interests of the state. His personality was now glorified out of all proportion, now denigrated just as immoderately.

Grigorovich realized that in view of the specific character of ballet he could not interfere with these historical disputes. He reasonably believed that today a straightforward approach to the theme would be irrelevant. Therefore he choreographed the ballet as a picturesque epic canvas with spectacular mass scenes, tragic monologues and lyrical duets.

The ballet had an element of philosophical parable, with a hero who was a mythical, almost folkloric personage. Grigorovich's main idea was to portray the emotional image of the epoch. Paradoxically, therefore, Tzar Ivan became more like Dostoyevsky's heroes and had features of intransigent religious bigotry and a mystical view of the world torn apart in a fierce struggle of passions and political ambitions. With this approach to the theme, Grigorovich lent special significance to the image of Anasthasia

Top, the great Soviet ballerina Marina Semenova with her pupils Natalia Bessmertnova (right) and Nina Sorokina. Bottom, Bessmertnova (second from right) begins her day with an hour of warm-up exercises in class.

Top, in rehearsal for *Ivan the Terrible*, 1975. Bottom, in rehearsal.

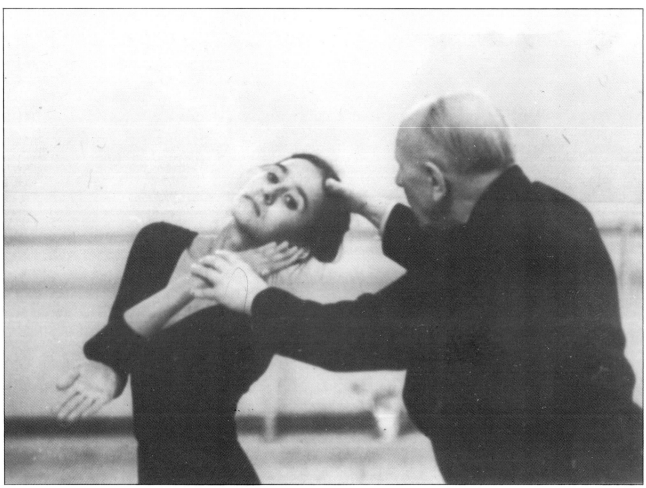

Top left, in rehearsal with the French dancer Mikael Dinar. Top right, with her pet dog, Fairy, in 1969. Bottom, with the famous Russian choreographer Kasyan Goleizovsky.

Top left, in rehearsal. Centre left, preparing for rehearsal. Bottom left, with Maya Plisetskaya (facing).

Top right, with Yuri Popko in 1982. Centre right, in rehearsal. Bottom right, with Alexander Bogatyrev.

Top left and bottom, rehearsing *Ivan the Terrible* with Yuri Grigorovich. Top right, rehearsing with Grigorovich.

Rehearsing *Romeo and Juliet* with Yuri Grigorovich.

As Anasthasia in *Ivan the Terrible*.

Top, with her former teacher, Sofia Golovkina, after the premiere of *Ivan the Terrible*. Bottom, dancing the role of Anasthasia in *Ivan the Terrible* with Irek Mukhamedov.

poisoned by the Tzar's boyar (or aristocratic) opponents. Her death causes a severe mental breakdown in the hero.

In Russian art this verion of the death of Anasthasia is traditionally accepted. But it is not known with certainty whether she was really murdered by the boyars or whether the idea that she was poisoned was simply the result of paranoia on the Tzar's part.

Tzar Ivan has no friends or associates, Anasthasia is his only loyal ally, who gives him the joy of love, consolation and support. She is like an angel of hope. They are surrounded by grim towers with the figures of jealous boyar traitors lurking between them. The Tzar is constantly haunted by apprehensions of an impending disaster. His palace with its phantom walls, his throne on which a dreaded imposter may appear at any moment — all is illusory and deprives him of peace of mind, inner harmony and confidence. From her first appearance to her death Anasthasia also seems a phantom, an apparition, a ghost. In the duet with Anasthasia the good sides of Ivan's nature and his human face are not yet deformed by his fury. The loss of Anasthasia, however, awakens the dormant forces of evil concealed in this demoniac figure.

The heroine personifies the Russian woman's character and the lyrical theme of the ballet, its truly national spirit seen in the free, fluid embodiment of the motifs of Russian icon-painting and Russian folklore. Anasthasia is the moral touchstone of the tragedy. Her death is a disaster not because she is a tzarina and Ivan's faithful wife, but because a gentle young woman dies, an innocent victim of a political plot in the corridors of power.

The scene of Anasthasia's death is the climax of the ballet. With timid surprise she watches the boyars surrounding her. With meek submission she performs her dance of death, not trying to run away from the inevitable. Parting with life, she does not accuse anybody. She slowly sinks to the floor, leaning against the sinister black plate that was her bed of love a short while ago. Her gaze is not one of pain or terror but of innocence and peaceful resignation to her fate.

In *Ivan the Terrible*, for the first time in Grigorovich's art, all events developed around a woman. In contrast to his earlier heroines, Anasthasia held an equal place in the hero's world of passions and emotions. She was a symbol of beauty purifying life, a defenceless creature just as frail as human life itself. She was trapped by human perfidy and crushed by the forces of history. Nevertheless, her life and her love, which were elusive and almost ephemeral, courageously opposed human malice and cruelty.

* * *

These were new intonations for Grigorovich: love challenged cruelty and love offered salvation from cruelty. Love was a strange and lonely islet in the violent ocean of life, a world engulfed by the flames of bloody feuds and torn apart by catastrophes.

The theme of love also prevailed in Grigorovich's two ballets that followed *Ivan the Terrible*: *The Angara* to music by Andrei Eshpai and *Romeo and Juliet* to music by Sergei Prokofiev. In each of the ballets of this original trilogy, the focus was a female character embodied by Natalia Bessmertnova.

'The chief motif of these ballets is one of tragic and fatal love,' Bessmertnova says. 'This is love that may end in death at any moment, a happiness that may be crushed by evil fate. In *Ivan the Terrible* the heroine dies. The hero dies in *The Angara*. In *Romeo and Juliet* both lovers die. In these ballets much was new to me, psychologically first and foremost.

'In each of my roles in these ballets the dramatic content was in the foreground. And each of them required a search for psychological development by means of dance.'

Indeed, in contrast to the choreographer's early productions, in these ballets he staged for Bessmertnova the theme of love was dominant. In each of them, the central concept was an ideal love match and man's lofty duty to cherish it as the supreme blessing of life.

It was not merely by chance that the key component in the 'trilogy' that united the choreographer and the ballerina was the adagio, while in the earlier ballets priority had invariably been given to the hero's dramatic monologue. Monologues, it is true, are also to be found in *Ivan the Terrible*, *The Angara* and *Romeo and Juliet*. But the climax of the first of these is Ivan's adagio with the dead Anasthasia, in *The Angara* adagios are also crucial to the action, and in *Romeo and Juliet* they determine all events — here every duet is like a short ballet in its own right.

Grigorovich's new interest in duets was provoked by Bessmertnova's distinctive style of dance and artistic manner, and by her instinctive attraction to the psychological adagio, in which she displayed a keen sense of empathy with her partner. In duets, indeed, Bessmertnova's skill is unequalled.

Juliet

Their next project was Romeo and Juliet. Grigorovich had long dreamt of staging a ballet on a Shakespearean theme. At first he had negotiated a production with the Kirov Ballet in Leningrad, but the pressure of work at the Bolshoi frustrated his plans. Then he received a proposal to stage Prokofiev's *Romeo and Juliet* at the Grand Opéra in Paris, where the premiere of *Ivan the Terrible*, with Bessmertnova dancing the part of Anasthasia, had made quite a hit in the autumn of 1976.

Grigorovich accepted the offer, and early in 1977 he started work on the choreography of the ballet in collaboration with soloists of the Bolshoi. He intended to go to Paris with complete if not finalized material. The part of Juliet was composed with Bessmertnova's distinctive style of dancing in mind. She danced it for the first time in the second premiere performance at the Grand Opéra in 1978, the French company having danced in the first performance.

They came back from Paris in a mood of disappointment. The success of the ballet with the theatre-going public was indisputable. Their colleagues had also commended it in superlative terms. The press, however, struck a discordant note. Critics had obviously expected a modernized interpretation of Shakespeare and took a dim view of Grigorovich's traditional romantic version. The choreographer had followed the guidelines set by the music composed in neo-romantic style which laid no claim to an absolutely new interpretation of the old story. At the time Prokofiev's music was taken with a pinch of salt, but today his ballet is a classic. And Grigorovich had staged it as a classic.

'The press praised the dancers,' Bessmertnova recalls, 'but I was none the better for that. Juliet was not just another run-of-the-mill part for me, but my own creation. And then it was a ballet created by a choreographer whose artistic outlook I had adopted as my own. I also knew that an ultramodern interpretation of Juliet would be at variance with my individual style. And then, Prokofiev's music is simply unfit for such interpretation.'

In the autumn Grigorovich started work on his production of *Romeo and Juliet* at the Bolshoi. He did so in the face of certain opposition from some ardent admirers of Lavrovsky's old version. In June 1979 the ballet had its first night at the Bolshoi.

Bessmertnova has never danced Ondine or Sylphide, classical images of romantic ballet. However, the image of Ondine, the prototype of all fantastic heroines of the past, has always been present invisibly in her art. In the part of Juliet it became strikingly manifest. Bessmertnova created the image of a girl existing on the boundary between reality and fantasy as an earthly yet incorporeal being. This boundary is elusive and lends a fantastic colour to Juliet in Bessmertnova's interpretation. Her aloofness and tragic incompatability with reality constitute the conflict of the role. It is only in its self-contained intimate world that this phantom feels happy, like a real human being of flesh and blood. Like a romantic naiad, Juliet is unable to live in a hostile world. One seems to see in her tragic dancing the brilliance of the magic wings of Sylphide that fall off when touched by a cruel hand.

Natalia's dancing in *Romeo and Juliet* is in purely romantic style. It is a contest between a weightless creature hovering in the air and the cruel forces of the earth. The tragedy of Romeo and Juliet develops in their private world. The choreographer has emphasized their isolation from real life in which they exist under duress, as it were, in a temporary and unsafe shelter, expecting a different life of eternal happiness.

Bessmertnova renounced all genre details of the character and presented an idealized Juliet, an image stylized to perfection. Only in the first episode, in Juliet's room, did she dance a merry and playful girl. Already in the ball scene, however, the image assumed a new dimension, and Juliet of the Renaissance turned into a fantastic Ondine, the heroine of romantic visions doomed by destiny to inevitable death.

Juliet summed up the theme revealed by the ballerina in Anasthasia and Valentina. These three roles cemented her close artistic union with Grigorovich.

Valentina

The Angara is a ballet on a modern Soviet theme based on

As Valentina in *The Angara* with Vladimir Vasilyev, 1976.

Alexei Arbuzov's once-popular play *The Irkutsk Story*. It tells of the tragic love of Valentina, a plain young woman who works as a shop cashier, for Sergei, a construction worker who gives his life to rescue children from drowning when the river Angara floods.

This story of a carefree young woman who has to come to terms with the shock of the tragedy and finds consolation in honest work was written in the late 1950s and has failed to outlast its day. Its events seem trivial today and its subject and stilted pathos much too melodramatic. But its theme of love was used by Grigorovich as the basis for a ballet production — with some essential revisions, of course. By expunging the genre details of the story, he produced a romantic love poem.

'For me Valentina differed little from the romantic heroines I had danced before,' Bessmertnova recalls. 'The theme of construction and reformation through work was certainly absent in the ballet. It would have destroyed its beauty. I danced a young woman's eternal desire for love and a quiet family life. Such things are understandable to any woman wherever she may live.'

Bessmertnova's Valentina was full of poetic charm and had a shade of mystery about her. The climax of her role was the final adagio of the hero and heroine, one of Grigorovich's most sincere creations, which she danced with full abandon — not detracting at all from her virtuoso skill.

The action of this adagio unfolds, as it were, in the heroine's imagination. She comes to the bank of the Angara, and Sergei's image floats into her mind. This is a duet of reminiscence in which the river, depicted by the corps de ballet, gradually floods the stage, enveloping the sad figure of Valentina. Sergei emerges from a group in the stage centre. He seems to be raised on the crest of the waves which lazily roll his body as if the river is reluctant to restore him to his beloved. This adagio, based on a theme of parting forever, is filled with a sensation of excruciating anguish. Valentina lulls her beloved to sleep, and the river takes up

Above, as Juliet in *Romeo and Juliet*, 1984.

As Juliet in *Romeo and Juliet* with Mikhail Lavrovsky, 1976.

As Juliet in *Romeo and Juliet* with Mikhail Gabovich, 1979.

Above, dancing the part of Juliet in *Romeo and Juliet* with Alexander Bogatyrev.

In rehearsal for *Romeo and Juliet* with Alexander Bogatyrev.

Above, dancing Rita in *The Golden Age*.

Above, as Rita in *The Golden Age* with Irek Mukhamedov.

Top, Natalia Bessmertnova thanks the conductor, Yuri Simonov, after the premiere of *The Golden Age*.
Bottom, curtain calls with Yuri Grigorovich after the premiere of *The Golden Age*, 1982.

Above, as Rita in *The Golden Age* with Gediminas Taranda as Jacques.

Above, in rehearsal for *The Golden Age* with Gediminas Taranda as Jacques.

As Rita in *The Golden Age* with Irek Mukhamedov as Boris.

As Rita in an adagio from *The Golden Age* with Irek Mukhamedov as Boris.

the motif of her lullaby. Her every step is timid and fearful, lest it disturb his eternal sleep.

The adagio is a pattern of supports and turns of the body in the air, long lines accentuating horizontal flight with a slow rhythm. Bessmertnova creates the image of a smoothly flowing river, enchanting with its steady motion.

This calls to mind another adagio from *Ivan the Terrible* where the hero weeps over Anasthasia, and she arises from her coffin dead and alive at the same time. Her lifeless body is a ghost, an apparition and at the same time a suffering spirit comforting her beloved and reconciling him to death. It is a spirit whose supplications, sighs and tears seem audible and palpable, a spirit that makes one feel an almost religious ecstasy, and yet it is also a sagging dead body.

The same effect is seen in the final adagio of *The Angara*. This is a dialogue with a dead beloved, a dialogue with death and nature, a young woman's reconciliation to the world that has crushed her hopes for happiness. Bessmertnova explains: 'To me the role of Valentina means a sensation of two conflicting elements — life and death. Life means love and motherhood, and death means the death of a dear human being, which makes one aware of life as a miracle and a challenge to death.'

Rita

The Golden Age, Dmitri Shostakovich's first ballet, composed in 1930, was resurrected by Grigorovich from the dead. At the time of its birth the ballet had been staged in Leningrad but proved a complete failure with the public. So it was quietly relegated to the archives, where it had staled for half a century. Its scenario was so poor that even the most enthusiastic lovers of Shostakovich's music could do nothing to help it.

For all the absurdity of the primitive plot, however, Shostakovich's music was excellent and was only distantly related to it. Reading some excerpts from the score, Grigorovich took note of this fact immediately.

'I wanted to save the music,' Grigorovich recalls. 'The composer, disappointed by the ballet's failure, preserved some pieces of the music by including them in his ballet suites, while other pieces were simply lost irretrievably. The score had to be restored from orchestral parts and fragments found by chance.'

Grigorovich wrote a new scenario in keeping with the genre and character of the music and borrowing from Shostakovich's other works. The original ballet had no lyrical theme, so the choreographer invented it.

The ballet is set in the USSR at the time of the New Economic Policy of the 1920s. *The Golden Age* is the name of a fashionable all-night cabaret club in which the heroine, Rita, is a dancer. The club shelters a gang of criminals led by Monsieur Jacques, a gallant thug who is Rita's partner in the show and is consumed by his passion for her. Rita for her part is in love with a young fisherman she has met at a street festival. The fisherman, Boris, symbolizes the new life; he is athletic and brave. Monsieur Jacques, his antagonist, robs banks and the self-indulgent bourgeois customers at the night club. Grigorovich preserved the general setting of the

social conflict of those years, but lent it a lyrical content leading the plot into the field of love poetry.

The part of Rita was specially choreographed for Natalia Bessmertnova. Nevertheless, she could not adapt to the part of a show dancer for quite some time; the character was entirely different from her earlier roles. At first, she danced Rita in her habitual style, so that she looked like a cross between Valentina and Juliet, but Grigorovich was dissatisfied with her efforts. He was being guided by a different logic and was searching for a more earthly heroine than those she had embodied in his earlier ballets.

'Indeed, it was hard for me to imagine myself a cabaret girl,' Bessmertnova says. 'I thought myself a purely romantic ballerina. I did not resist my role, of course, but at times I felt it was so alien as not to be taken seriously.' She sensed hidden implications in the character, however, and she went into its genre details more thoroughly than she had ever done before.

'Unlike my former roles, in which I was guided by my general idea of the character and made no deliberate effort to unravel its psychology, Rita was a more concrete person who lived in my own time and faced problems a real actress may have in real life,' she says. 'The life of an actress has two different sides: one is her simple and natural daily life, the other is her life on the stage under the floodlights in front of a large audience. If these sides are in harmony, she is happy. Rita was torn by a conflict between her natural desire for love and happiness and her duty to pander to the base instincts of her cabaret clients.'

Indeed, the ballet is symbolic, suggesting the image of a theatre whose actors cheat their audience of foppish pleasure-hunters. The heroine hates her job and dreams of a different life, honest and natural, like the one led by the young fisherman and his friends.

This was the dramatic line the ballerina followed in her dance. It is a dance of contrasts: her free dance at the festival and her sensual dance in the cabaret which shamelessly sells her feminine charm for cash. She feels herself an alien in The Golden Age club and reveals her true self in her lyrical adagio with the hero. Her amazing cantilena dancing leaves the audience spellbound — it is a declaration of love that seems to last forever.

But she is unable to break with the life of the cabaret at once. It has been part of her own life for a long time. Her last tango with her show partner is a mixture of passion and despair in which she defiantly dons the mask of a show girl.

The ballet has a happy ending, however — the first in Grigorovich's ballets. The heroine finds her way to a happy life in harmony with nature and herself.

The drama and tragedy of the art of great ballerinas of the past was rooted in the conflict between their devotion to the theatre and the desire for earthly happiness natural to any human being. Love in ballet was always a dream or an unattainable ideal which leads to inevitable death. This dramatic conflict mirrored the conflicts in the dancers' lives.

Bessmertnova has conveyed this reflection of a ballerina's life in many of her parts. The best is Rita in *The Golden Age*. The heroine has finally won her right to a happy finale.

Top left, as Odile in *Swan Lake* with Alexander Bogatyrev. Top right and bottom, as Odette in *Swan Lake*.

As Odette in *Swan Lake*.

CHAPTER FIVE

Classics

In classical ballet Natalia Bessmertnova has attained the pinnacle of artistry in the parts of Odette-Odile, Raymonda and Giselle. In each of them she has been an innovator, presenting a totally new interpretation.

Odette-Odile

Bessmertnova first danced in *Swan Lake* as far back as 1965, in a traditional version of the ballet. Grigorovich's version had its premiere at the Bolshoi on 25 December 1969. Here her creativity, talent and virtuosity revealed themselves in a new light, although the choreography of her part had not undergone substantial changes.

In the new version, the ballerina danced a new conceptual image of Odette-Odile based on an integral interpretation of the music. 'The guideline I follow in my dance is suggested by the emotional message of the scene, by the music rather than the plot.' This is the gist of her innovative interpretation of this canonized role.

At one time the manner of performance and the interpretation of the 'white' act of *Swan Lake* were strongly influenced by the ideas of dramatic ballet. The ballerina was required to create a concrete image of Odette turned into a swan by sorcery. She was expected to accentuate in her dance elements imitating a swan's movements and poses. The Dying Swan of Pavlova and Fokine is an example in point.

In twentieth-century Russian ballet the traditions of dancing the part of Odette can be traced to Marina Semenova and Galina Ulanova. Semenova gave the role heroic traits, presenting a character aspiring to freedom. Ulanova emphasized the lyrical and psychological line, presenting a lifelike emotional image.

On the Bolshoi stage a vivid interpretation was given by Maya Plisetskaya, a ballerina of exotic style with a picturesque fluid language. Her Odette was reminiscent of Semenova's in spirit, but Plisetskaya imparted to the image more striking colours, at times almost naturalistic.

Bessmertnova gave up the genre, psychological, naturalistic and pictorial details of her predecessors in her interpretation and boldly renounced the habitual dramatic conflict in the ballet. 'My idea', she says, 'was to express in dance emotions consonant with the music. These emotions were to shape a psychological character that would not be tied in with the plot. The image of Odette is usually split into fragments: her fearfulness, her anxiety, her trustfulness . . . . I didn't feel like acting out individual emotional states and following the logic of their transition. I was interested in a common motif and an integral image not broken up into small components.'

Bessmertnova's Odette dwells in an unreal world. Siegfried is an 'alien', and she regards him with surprise and timid curiosity. In Tchaikovsky's original she is a good fairy, close to human beings but elusive like a phantom. Bessmertnova sensed this image in the music. She is a fairy swan frightened by Siegfried's sudden intrusion that has disturbed her solitary world. Her life in captivity is fun and pleasurable to her, because she is unaware of any other life beyond the limits of her lake. Bessmertnova has created the image of an enchanted fairy who does not suffer under Rothbart's rule at all. Siegfried's impassioned calls, however, excite her interest in a world different from her own; she is no longer happy with her monotonous life, and the faultless beauty of her lake now seems sterile and boring to her. Siegfried's coming to the lake has stirred her desire to experience the joy of a different life.

With this conceptual image of Odette, the ballerina's transition to the black swan, Odile, is perfectly logical. This interpretation has an impeccable expression in dance. In the second (swan) scene of the ballet the dancing is amazingly graceful. It is an endless play of lines and poses following a fanciful pattern. She is irresistibly seductive in this display of her feminine charms.

The third act (Odile in Tchaikovsky's original) was the climax of Bessmertnova's performance. Odile's first appearance at the ball stunned the audience. Her eyes shining in triumph and the deathly pallor of her face made her a living ghost seized with impatience. Her excitement in anticipation of the ball erupted in her swift vigorous leaps that carried her seemingly weightless body across the stage. Her evil was concealed under the mask of her angelic face. The demoniac forces of her spirit longed for carnal love. All of it, however, was just a piece of acting for its own sake. She delighted in the ease of her triumph.

In the final scene — the storm on the lake, when the Prince comes to beg forgiveness — Bessmertnova's Odette-Odile also follows her own logic, trying not so much to forgive the sin committed by Siegfried as to expiate her own. In Grigorovich's first version she dies saving the Prince from certain death, because in the choreographer's conception Rothbart has no intention of destroying Odette. His target is Siegfried, who has disturbed the harmony of his swan kingdom. The later version of the ballet has a happy ending, though not very conclusive. Bessmertnova has preserved the motif of saving her unintended victim (the motif of Giselle). The story of Odette-Odile in Bessmertnova's interpretation is a story of love — reckless, passionate and proud — rejecting her admirer yet ready to protect him at a fatal moment.

Raymonda

In June 1984 Bessmertnova danced the part of Raymonda in Alexander Glazunov's ballet of the same name which had

Dancing the title role in *Raymonda* with Alexander Bogatyrev.

been revived on the Bolshoi stage by Grigorovich. The ballerina's most recent work, it closely followed Rita in *The Golden Age*, a ballet that had been the highest point in her artistic progress and determined the integrity and logic of her path in ballet.

After the premiere of *The Golden Age* Natalia felt like taking time off to collect her thoughts and make new plans for the future. She therefore took a lukewarm interest in Grigorovich's new work on *Raymonda*. She was familiar with all earlier versions of *Raymonda*, and all of them seemed psychologically incoherent to her. The part of Raymonda was picturesque, of course, but it lacked profundity of meaning.

On reflection, however, Bessmertnova decided to join in the choreographer's work and after a few rehearsals came up with a complete and absolutely original interpretation of Raymonda, relying on the experience of her latest modern roles rather than her portrayals of classical parts such as Aurora or Odette.

Grigorovich had discerned in Petipa's conception the main idea: *Raymonda* is a ballet about a woman's destiny. His version was a logical extension of the themes he had pursued in *Ivan the Terrible*, *The Angara* and *The Golden Age*, though on a different plane. He preserved the style and colours of the *Raymonda* of Petipa and filled it with youthful energy.

Natalia Bessmertnova danced in this world-famous *chef d'oeuvre* of Glazunov and Petipa after a series of premieres in modern productions. In this classical ballet, which is a gruelling test of dancing skill for any ballerina, she demonstrated her graceful virtuosity based on the advantages of the academic school, as well as her superlative artistry which lends venerated classics the charm of innovation.

She created an image unknown in the history of Raymonda — a part for which her great predecessors, each in her own way, had come up with variations on a theme of regal feminine beauty proudly and dispassionately guarding itself against sin and emanating the cool light of untarnished chastity. True, the earlier versions of this ballet had offered little material, if any, for a different interpretation. The part of Raymonda had always been valued primarily for its wealth of dancing which allowed a ballerina to display the broad range of her technique and brilliant virtuosity. Yuri Grigorovich's new version, in contrast, had great depth of meaning and subtlety that were revealed by Bessmertnova with unmistakable faithfulness to his conception.

The choreographer revived the ballet without going against Petipa's version in any way. In fact, he restored its original choreography in a more complete production, with long-forgotten episodes and details unearthed from archives. He had made a thorough study of the original and found some twists and turns of the story that had never been identified before. He accentuated them in the old choreography and developed them in the additional new dances and details he had invented himself, weaving them into the structure of Petipa's classical version.

For instance, the dances which had always existed in the first scene now included among their performers Ray-

As Raymonda with Alexander Bogatyrev.

monda's fiancé, the gallant knight Jean de Brienne. This scene was now interpreted as a farewell to his beloved before his departure for the next Crusade. In former productions Jean de Brienne had left for a battle against the Saracens and had not been present on the stage for most of the action.

In the dances of the second act, which were also in the classical version, Abderakhman, a Saracen sheik who seeks Raymonda's love, has a fuller part to perform too. In the earlier versions it was simply pantomime, but in this version both lyrical heroes have learned the language of dance and assumed images and characters nonexistent in the former interpretations that doomed them to inaction. What was a festive production full of pomp in which Raymonda had nothing to do but guard her virtue was transformed by Grigorovich into a lyrical story in which each of the characters displays a drama of emotions.

This psychological conflict, which was a novelty in the stage life of *Raymonda*, was conveyed in Bessmertnova's dancing with exceptional sincerity. She breathed new life into old adagios and variations, and added Grigorovich's inventions to them with great stylistic precision to achieve an integral and continuous development of Raymonda's personality. Her talented interpretation threw into salient relief the difference between *The Sleeping Beauty* and *Raymonda* — two ballets which had often been imagined to be closely affined.

The new choreography of *Raymonda* was consonant with Bessmertnova's emotional make-up and the style and character of her dancing. The story of Raymonda now

As Giselle.

suggested broad associations, echoing the romantic images danced by Bessmertnova and her own theme of a ballerina's destiny as a woman and an actress.

Bessmertnova's Raymonda is a perfect revelation of this theme. Her heroine lives in constant expectation of change, makes a mysterious journey into a world of beautiful dreams, experiences wonderful moments of sensual temptation and learns about the inner world of a woman's soul. This is a ballet about a woman's awakening to love, and about dangers that may destroy the harmony of her essential inner balance between self-control and the powerful emotions of love.

Raymonda's dancing is a whirlwind of passion that carries her towards the alluring realm of sensual pleasure and makes her forget the dangers of the world, embodied by the Oriental Prince Abderakhman. His death at the hands of Jean de Brienne returns her to reality. Bessmertnova's brilliant dancing of Raymonda's variations revealed superbly the evolution of this character, the lyrical theme of the ballet and its conflict in which true love triumphs over its carnal fake.

Giselle

Natalia Bessmertnova's art is virtually epitomized by the part of Giselle. She first danced it at the age of twenty two, as its first performer, Carlotta Chrisi, had done. Before Bessmertnova, three great ballerinas had presented their own distinctive interpretations of Giselle on the Russian stage: Anna Pavlova, who revealed the motif of a woman's self-sacrifice and the triumph of love over death; Olga

Spesivtseva, whose Giselle was a symbol of dying beauty in an era of social upheavals; and Galina Ulanova, who relied on Pavlova's interpretation but also gave the image of Giselle salient features of lifelikeness, against a background of acute social conflict in which the noble spirit and moral integrity of the peasant girl contrasted sharply with the carefree and profligate life of the young aristocrat Albert.

Bessmertnova's very first performance of Giselle had a clear, neat and quite original conception of the most important aspect of the role — the dual image of a plain girl in the first act and a fantastic wilis in the second. Her predecessors had often failed to strike the right balance to bring integrity to the image; they usually based their roles on contrasts, emphasizing the isolation of the second act from the first.

'In my dancing I followed my intuition, and I sensed no big difference between Giselle the human being and Giselle the wilis,' Bessmertnova explains. 'I remember that I liked the second act better.' She was thus rather indifferent to the lifelike image in the first act, restoring to *Giselle* its romantic poetry, renouncing lifelike details and the motif of disillusionment with her unfaithful beloved. The events of Giselle's love affair with Albert were unimportant; the theme of 'love betrayed' which had been traditional with almost all performers of Giselle was boldly discarded.

Giselle has a mystery known to her alone: she was born to dance. Throughout the first act she seeks to realize her destiny. The second act sees her consecration as a wilis. She longs to join the ever-dancing brides. For Bessmertnova the key motivation in *Giselle* is this passion for dance. It is the main motif of the ballet, linking what seem at first glance to be two separate acts and blending reality and fantasy.

Indeed, what else but dance, which constitutes the leitmotif of the ballet, integrates the act of real life with the act of fantasy? It is in dance that Giselle is in her element from her first appearance on stage. Dance is the cause of all events, all joys and sorrows. Dance can kill, and dance can save life.

Bessmertnova's Giselle is a graceful, subtle and artistic character prone to capricious changes of moods, charmingly carefree, spontaneous and emotional. The clue to the true meaning of the role lies in the character of the heroine, her artistic emotional make-up, and the conflict between her earthly affection for another human being and her infatuation with her heavenly art of dance.

The second act of *Giselle* is one of Bessmertnova's finest creations. One reason is that the style of the choreography is in organic harmony with her physique: the long lines and perfect proportions of her body correspond to the requirements of romantic aesthetics and the romantic style of dance. It would be wrong, however, to consider this the sole reason for her success. The other main reason is that she interprets the ballet within the framework of her own lyrical story, which unexpectedly reveals the genuine poetic message of the ballet and the romantic outlook on the world which gave birth to this story of love and dance: Giselle learns that art is impossible without human feeling and human passion. An artist translates the suffering of the soul

Left, as Giselle. Above, in the madness scene from *Giselle.*

As Giselle with Mikael Dinar at the Grand Opéra in Paris.

Top, with Mikhail Lavrovsky in the pas de deux from the first act of *Giselle*. Bottom, in her dressing room after her debut as Giselle.

Dancing the title role in *Giselle* with Alexander Bogatyrev.

Above left, as Giselle with Alexander Bogatyrev. Above right, in her dressing room after performing Giselle.

Left, as Giselle. Above, after the presentation of the
Grand Prix in Amsterdam for Giselle, 1968.

Dancing the heroine in *Giselle* with Mikhail Lavrovsky.

into a consummate work of art. She is different from the other wilis: her dance is a dance of resurrection, while theirs is a dance of death. Her revolt against the wilis constitutes the conflict of the second act.

Giselle was a milestone in Bessmertnova's career. It brought to light the main motives of her art, her love of poetical generalization ignoring the temptation to merely tell a story offered by a concrete plot.

Partners

'Relations with a partner in ballet', Bessmertnova says, 'are quite unlike those in drama or films, for obvious reasons. The degree of dependence on each other is immeasurably greater. I have danced with very different partners. My permanent partners have been few. In my early period in ballet it was mostly Mikhail Lavrovsky, then Alexander Bogatyrev, and in recent times Irek Mukhamedov, a young newcomer at the Bolshoi.'

The Bessmertnova-Lavrovsky duo was admired for its inimitable sincerity. Lavrovsky will be remembered as the most sincere Bolshoi dancer, temperamental and impulsive. Bessmertnova has danced Giselle, Shirin, Phrygia, Masha and Odette with him. A classical dancer of romantic and tragic roles, Lavrovsky continues the finest traditions of Russian ballet.

In the same years Bessmertnova occasionally danced with Nikolai Fadeyechev, Maris Liepa and Vladimir Tikhonov. Thanks to her amazing sense of partnering she easily found a common language with each of them, and they formed partnerships of remarkable harmony.

'I never take advantage of my partner but try to be in rapport with him,' the ballerina says. 'Indeed, the artistic impression of dance depends on combined effort. So I always treat my partners as equals, although some of them are better than others, of course. Work in concert matters most to me. All the more so as in Grigorovich's ballets duets are sometimes more important than solo dancing.'

In the 1970s Bessmertnova and Lavrovsky's artistic paths diverged. And soon the elegant, handsome and chivalrous Alexander Bogatyrev became her invariable partner in classical ballets. The athletic and manly virtuoso Irek Mukhamedov, who joined the company relatively recently, is her steady partner in the modern repertoire. With him, she has danced Phrygia in *Spartacus*, Anasthasia in *Ivan the Terrible* and Rita in *The Golden Age*. She has, in fact, danced with all leading soloists of the Bolshoi, including Vladimir Vasilyev, who was her partner in *Ivan the Terrible* and in the premiere of *The Angara*.

'I find it fascinating to dance with different partners not only in different roles but in the same role as well,' Bessmertnova says. 'A new partner gives me pep, making me change something in my own dance which assumes new intonations. For instance, for a long time I was the only performer of the part of Anasthasia, while my partners who danced Ivan were different dancers. And today I dance Anasthasia with Irek Mukhamedov or Yuri Vladimirov.'

In rehearsal with Mikhail Lavrovsky.

Above, being congratulated by Galina Ulanova after a performance of the Lavrovsky production of *Romeo and Juliet*, 1974.

A poster for *The Golden Age*.

Above, receiving the Lenin Komsomol Prize. Left to right, Ekaterina Maximova, Nina Sorokina, Natalia Bessmertnova.

Being awarded the Anna Pavlova Prize of the French Academy of Dance by Serge Lifare, 1977.

Above, being made an honourable citizen of Hamilton, Canada in 1979.

Curtain calls with Mikhail Lavrovsky after a performance of *The Angara.*

Top, at London Zoo. Bottom, Natalia (right) with her sister Tatiana (centre) and Bolshoi ballerina Lyudmilla Prokofieva (left).

Top, Natalia Bessmertnova. Bottom, with her husband, Yuri Grigorovich, in the Anna Pavlova museum in London.

Above, a party at the Grigorovichs' after the premiere of *The Golden Age*, 1982. Left to right, Irek Mukhamedov, Yuri Grigorovich, Natalia Bessmertnova, Tatiana Golikova, Gediminas Tazanda.

Top, Natalia's mother and nephew, Misha, outside their summer cottage. Bottom, Natalia with Misha.

In Mexico in 1984.

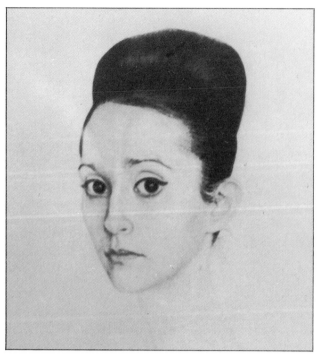

Above left, in 1978. Above right, portrait painted in the USA by the artist Boris Chaliapin, son of the famous Russian singer Fedor Chaliapin.

At home with her husband, Yuri Grigorovich.

Epilogue

Natalia Bessmertnova is known for her modesty. She has an ironic attitude towards chasing after fame. She does not take part in ultra-modern, synthetic productions or take much interest in experiments for their own sake. She carefully avoids being in the focus of public curiosity and sensation of any kind. In her life and work she is a serious person concentrating on her daily duties — dancing the whole of the Bolshoi's enormous classical and modern repertoire.

Marina Semenova, famous as a Bolshoi star of the mid-1920s, calls her the First Ballerina of the Bolshoi, who will go down in ballet history as a dancer with unique individuality. 'She lives on the stage. Her lyricism and romantic inspiration are just as youthful as ever. Her psychological penetration is highly intelligent, and her virtuoso skill is on a par with the world's best. She is the Soviet Union's pride.'

Bessmertnova's coach Rimma Karelskaya testifies: 'Bessmertnova has an extraordinary muscular memory. She can immediately respond to a word in dance. I don't know another ballerina who so painstakingly analyses any flaw in her performance. No stereotype is good for coaching her. Much depends on her mood; she may easily lose her temper or withdraw into herself. She is very scrupulous in work. In the choreography of her parts she is a stickler for accuracy.'

In Bessmertnova's own view three factors matter most to her in dance: first, the intrinsic harmony of the choreographic score; second, the beauty of the music; and third, freedom of improvisation. By this she does not mean improvisation in the ordinary sense, of course. 'I always dance what is planned in my role,' she says. 'But I hate fixed nuances, and each time I dance, I dance differently. I rely on my feel for dance.

'I cannot help it,' she admits ruefully. 'I'm really much too susceptible to a change in my mood. Unlike many other dancers, I never divide my role into primary and secondary elements, such as accentuating a movement here and making a pause there. It simply doesn't come off if I try.'

After rehearsing the old version of *Giselle* with Bessmertnova, Leonid Lavrovsky said: 'It's a pleasure to work with her, but it's also very difficult. She can only do what she understands and accepts.' In effect, this means that Bessmertnova's every performance is unique. It is a blend of spontaneity with a filigree classical skill.

Bessmertnova has starred in all Grigorovich's ballets of the last two decades. The ballerina believes that their artistic union has proved so fruitful for a special reason: 'Grigorovich has an inborn sense of veracity in dance. That is, he feels unmistakably what is true and what is untrue in it. Therefore, no element of dancing comes out false or unnatural. And then, he is extremely sensitive to the dancer's individual style. He adapts to the logic suggested by the dancer's body and physical potential. His intuition never betrays him. This has always excited my interest in working with this choreographer.'

Bessmertnova remembers all her coaches with gratitude. 'My first coach was Galina Ulanova, though for a short time. Then Marina Semenova coached me for many years. She was followed by Nikolai Simachev and Rimma Karelskaya. Marina Semenova has again been with me for much of the time recently.

'A coach is not the architect of a role but the engineer who builds it. Learning new roles takes up most of the time in a stage career. Another person's fresh look at the dancer and long experience are very important for success. For instance, I rehearsed Raymonda with Semenova, who had danced that part brilliantly at the former Marinsky Theatre. Although I danced it in my own way, her help with the interpretation was invaluable.'

The veteran US impressario Sol Hurok, who at one time sponsored Anna Pavlova and Fedor Chaliapin's triumphant world tours, as well as the Bolshoi Ballet's performances in America, had this to say about Bessmertnova's dancing: 'An impressario is not a prophet, but he will get nowhere if he cannot look ahead. Once I saw a charming girl at the Moscow Ballet School and predicted a great future for her. After a few years, during the Bolshoi's guest tour she became America's favourite .... Now, I believe, she is the world's best ballerina. This is Natalia Bessmertnova.'

The art of Natalia Bessmertnova has been applauded by ballet lovers in more than twenty countries around the world. She is a winner of the prestigious State Prize of the USSR, a gold medallist at the Varna Ballet Contest, and one of the few ballerinas awarded the Anna Pavlova Prize by the Paris Academy of Dance, for her performance of Giselle.

Curtain calls with Yuri Grigorovich.